Bellamy's Changing World: The Forest
was conceived, edited and designed
by Frances Lincoln Limited
Apollo Works, 5 Charlton Kings Road, London NW5 2SB

First published in Great Britain by
Macdonald and Co. (Publishers) Ltd,
Greater London House,
Hampstead Road,
London NW1 7RX
A BPCC plc Company

British Library Cataloguing in Publication Data

Bellamy, David, *1933* –
The forest — (Bellamy's Changing World: 1)
1. Forest ecology — Juvenile literature
I. Title   II. Dow, Jill   III. Series
574.909'52   QH541.5.F6

ISBN 0-356-13567-5

Printed and bound in Italy

Design and Art Direction Debbie Mackinnon

Frances Lincoln Ltd. would like to thank
Pippa Rubinstein, Trish Burgess, Sarah Mitchell,
Kathy Henderson, Kathryn Cave, Stephen Pollock
and Jackie Westbrook for help with the series.

Bellamy's Changing World

The
Forest

David Bellamy

with illustrations by Jill Dow

Macdonald

It's a fine spring day and the forest is full of life. In some areas, foresters are working: felling trees and planting new ones to provide paper pulp, timber and firewood for the world outside. Here, some visitors have found a beautiful place for a picnic under a huge oak tree.

The oak is very old and is like a world in itself. High on its branches, the rooks feed their nestlings. A woodpecker drills into a dead branch to find grubs to eat, and a squirrel, who was busy eating the leaf buds, chases away a great tit. Even the yellow fungus is feeding on the dead wood.

Every year the old tree grows new bark, wood and leaves. These provide food for a host of different insects like shield bugs, caterpillars and leaf miners. It's a good thing that the birds like to eat these insects or there would be far too many and they could kill the trees.

Roller caterpillars hide from the birds by wrapping themselves up in the leaves while they turn into moths. Some insects lay their eggs in the softer parts of the buds, leaves and twigs. The tree then grows a lump or gall around the eggs, which protects them till they hatch. Broad-leaved trees like the oak are the only place in which many of these creatures can make their home.

1 shield bug   2 leaf miner   3 oak bush cricket   4 roller caterpillar
5 hairstreak caterpillar   6 oak flowers   7 gall wasp
8 oak-apple gall   9 marble gall   10 spangle gall

More small creatures live among the mosses and lichens on the oak tree's trunk. Millions of tiny green plants cover the side of the trunk where the rainwater runs down, and the tree creeper climbs up this green carpet hunting for insects. On the other side, the lace-web spider sits by her trap waiting for something to drop in, and the long-legged harvestmen hunt among the moss. The peppered moth is nearly invisible against the bark.

The bark protects the trunk and branches and gives a firm foothold for all the mosses and lichens, while ferns and other plants root in the cracks. As the tree grows taller and broader, the old bark splits and new layers grow to fill the cracks.

High up the wood pigeon is sitting tight on her eggs. She knows that squirrels like to eat eggs and even baby birds.

It's nearly midsummer and the oak is unfolding a new crop of juicy young leaves. The old ones have been eaten by so many insects that they are in tatters. The cushions of moss clinging to the bark have grown capsules on delicate stalks. When the capsules are ripe they open, releasing thousands of spores which blow onto other twigs and bare bark, where they grow into new moss plants.

Under the trees it is cool and shady, even in midsummer. A young deer comes to graze on the fresh green grass. Most of the plants already bear fruits and seeds. They flowered in spring before the leaves shut out the sunlight. Last year's fallen leaves have almost disappeared. Pulled underground and eaten by earthworms, they enrich the soil. The acorns have gone too, all except one which has taken root beneath its parent tree. At first the seedling fed on its fat acorn. Now, its new leaves make their own food from the dappled sunlight that filters down. It grows very slowly, but one day, if it survives, it could take the place of one of the giant old forest oaks, felled by a storm or for timber. Not all acorns grow up into trees: if they did there would soon be no room in the forest.

At night, when the forest is dark and mysterious to us, wood mice are out looking for fallen acorns to store away for winter. One is just about to nibble the top off the oak seedling, but the hungry owl, with its enormous eyes that allow it to see so well in the dark, has spotted the mouse and is swooping down . . . The forest can be a dangerous place for mice as well as seedlings.

Bats cannot see as well as owls, but they do have very good hearing. They find their way around by using the echoes of their own high-pitched squeaks to warn them of the position of trees and other objects.

In the undergrowth glow worms use light to signal to their mates. The honey fungus glows too, but we don't know why it does.

In autumn there is plenty of food around, but winter is not far away. The fallen leaves are white with last night's frost. The toads have found a safe place under the leaves to spend the winter. The mice have stocked their burrows with food and grass for nests. The squirrels are out collecting acorns and toadstools: they know which toadstools are safe to eat.

We can only see the umbrella or bracket of the toadstool —
that's the part that sticks up into the air. But underneath the
fallen leaves, tiny root-like threads spread out and feed on
dead material, helping it to rot down. Toadstools help to
keep the forest tidy and the soil fertile. Without them the
trees would soon be buried in dead leaves and twigs.

On a sunny day in late winter the forest stirs in its winter sleep. The bats hang silently in the hollow trunk and the squirrels are hidden in their untidy drey of leaves and twigs, but a winter moth is out enjoying the sunshine. People are busy in the forest too and the foresters' saws can be heard in the distance. A tortoiseshell butterfly has been tempted out by the sun. But will it be able to find the flowers it needs to feed on?

A fieldfare and a blackbird have come to eat the ripe black fruits of the ivy that clings to the tree trunk. Higher up, a mistle thrush pecks at the berries of the mistletoe which roots deep into the tree's wood to draw its sap. Nearby, deer graze around hazel trees already covered with catkins, sending clouds of yellow pollen onto the wind. The oak tree itself will not flower until spring, though the fat buds promise a good crop of leaves and acorns to come.

But the giant oak and its companions will never see another spring or autumn. They have been cut down and sold for timber and now new trees are being planted in their place. These new trees are conifers. The landowners like them because they grow much faster than the broad-leaved trees and produce their harvest of wood more quickly. But what about all the plants and creatures that lived in and around the oak?

All that's left is a stump showing 202 growth rings – one ring for each year of the oak's life – and a pile of logs. The ground is churned up and most of the wildlife has fled. Only a few damp-loving plants, like rushes, are thriving, and the jackdaws are busy collecting twigs for their nests nearby.

In time, some creatures, like deer, come into the new plantation to feed on the grass, bilberries and ferns growing between the young trees. But as the trees get bigger, few plants are able to grow under their dense shade. The needles, when they fall, are so tough that they rot very slowly; the worms avoid them and the soil becomes poorer. The jackdaws and the squirrels – including some red squirrels – soon settle in, but many of the other creatures will have moved to other parts of the forest, or will have died.

With few birds to eat them, pine shoot beetles burrow freely into the tender new twigs and looper caterpillars and greenfly attack the young needles. The trees are in danger from these harmful pests, although the ladybirds help by eating some of the greenfly. The foresters use a helicopter to spray the plantation with chemicals to kill the insects – unfortunately they can kill ladybirds too.

This part of the plantation is older.
The tall straight spruce trees will make
a fine crop of timber and they provide a
home for some beautiful animals and birds.

The colourful crossbills
use their specially shaped beaks to
prise the seeds out of the cones, while the
crested tits feed their young in a hole in the tree.
They have to watch out for the goshawk hunting
between the trees and for the sleek pine marten
which will eat almost anything it can catch. Below
them, a pine hawk moth rests on the trunk, and
under the trees, where little grows, the wood ants
pile the dead needles up into nests.

The foresters have fixed bat boxes to the trees to
encourage bats to use the wood. They have also
built a tall observation tower, from which they can
watch over the plantation and keep an eye open for
trouble, especially fire.

The view from the tower is breathtaking. The forest ranger is up here, talking about how the forest works and about the problems of raising a crop that takes so long to grow before it is ready for harvest. He points out the purple emperor butterflies and the squirrels up in the tops of the trees.

Plantations of spruce, larch and pines are dotted about but willow, oak and alder have been allowed to grow along the river, providing a home for many of the plants, insects and animals that would once have lived around the old oak. A grassy clearing around its stump is now used as a picnic site. People come here for the new nature trail and to enjoy everything that the different kinds of forest have to offer.

MEETHILL SCHOOL
PETERHEAD
ABERDEENSHIRE

the old

the observation tower